D0044761

Axel Lindén

counting
sheep

Reflections and Observations
of a Swedish Shepherd

ATRIA BOOKS

New York   London   Toronto   Sydney   New Delhi

ATRIA
BOOKS

An Imprint of Simon & Schuster, Inc.
1230 Avenue of the Americas
New York, NY 10020

First Atria Books hardcover edition November 2018

ATRIA BOOKS and colophon are trademarks of Simon & Schuster, Inc.

For information about special discounts for bulk purchases, please
contact Simon & Schuster Special Sales at 1-866-506-1949 or
business@simonandschuster.com.

The Simon & Schuster Speakers Bureau can bring authors to your
live event. For more information, or to book an event, contact the
Simon & Schuster Speakers Bureau at 1-866-248-3049 or visit our
website at www.simonspeakers.com.

Interior design by Amy Trombat

Manufactured in the United States of America

10 9 8 7 6 5 4 3 2 1

Library of Congress Cataloging-in-Publication Data has been applied for.

ISBN 978-1-9821-0062-9
ISBN 978-1-9821-0063-6 (ebook)

Introduction

It feels rather long ago now, the time we lived in Stock-holm. Initially we thought of the move out to the country, to my parents' farm, as a project, as a period when we would be doing something different. Maybe even as a longer kind of holiday. Several of my colleagues at university, where I taught literary studies, had received a grant of some kind to do research abroad for a couple of years after completing their doctorates. That sort of thing.

At that time there were several of us who became aware of the environmental crisis and the impending catastrophe. What's going to happen when water fails to come out of taps, electricity from plugs, or cash from dispensers? I was also starting to think about global patterns of resource flows. I realized, of course, that the world was unfair, but I hadn't really thought about the direct connection between high and low standards of living. The conclusion I drew, a bit hastily perhaps, was that the only way to seriously tackle the threat to the climate and global injustice, while also making sure of the bare necessities when it all came tumbling down, was to start growing our own food and chopping our own wood. And getting some sheep.

The whole idea was completely absurd in the situation I found myself in back then. I lived in a flat, commuted to work, pretended to be aware by going to political meetings and vegan restaurants. The best thing we could come up with when we used to talk about making a difference was to write an article or start a Facebook group. My colleagues and I might convince ourselves that we barely contributed anything at all to economic growth and consumption. Although this sounded a bit hollow when the salaries we received were spent in full on luxuries and indulgences.

But there was something that appealed even more. A vague and yet powerful feeling. I wanted out. To be outside. In Stockholm, I was like an indoor cat. Everything I needed was in packages, served up in boxes of one kind or another. I had been domesticated and made passive, never experiencing any immediate contact with the elements. I never really needed to know what the weather would be like. Suddenly I wanted to be out there, feeling the cold in my fingers, hitting myself on the thumb, and wearing my trousers out at the knees.

This feeling was exacerbated by placing the children in a kindergarten on the other side of the inner city. We had to travel by tube (subway) for forty minutes every morning and again in the afternoon. The children lay down on their backs along the aisle floor. They were simply exhausted by the situation. It made me think: We don't belong here. We've got to get out.

As if by divine intervention our moving plans coincided with my parents wanting to leave their farm. My parents' farm seemed to be the perfect combination of individual family homes, vegetable gardens, paddocks, and agricultural buildings within one commune. At the beginning of the twentieth century the farm had been a kind of miniature feudal society. In addition to the buildings used for agricultural ends, a number of homes had been built for the people who worked on the farm. With the restructuring of the agricultural sector, the feudal lord had become just another small businessman, the dwellings were turned into housing associations, and the huge cowshed with the magnificent round barn (a peculiar construction that looked like a combination of Shakespeare's Globe and a pagan cathedral) became an abandoned museum object.

The idea was that we would occupy the old core of the farm. The big fields and the cowsheds could be rented out. We took over the tenancies of some of the houses and created an oasis of non-mechanical small-scale agriculture in the midst of the high-tech, fossil-fueled landscape of modern farming.

All our friends back in the city, the ones who lived on the same tube line, were convinced we would soon be back. But it was too late. We're sheep farmers and country people now. When I lived in Stockholm my mother used to be appalled by all the noise, the hustle and bustle. It couldn't be good for the children. . . . I would roll my eyes, thinking she was a stick-in-the-mud. Now I'm appalled by life in the big city as well. It can't be good for anyone.

Toward the end of that first summer, my wife and I were looking over the hedge at the big fields one warm evening. We had labored all day at harvesting root vegetables. We had gathered enough to feed a family for an entire year. From one crop. Huge headlights were sweeping across the fields out there. They were coming toward us. A whooshing and subtly complex sound was getting louder. A gigantic combine harvester swept past us in a disdainful pirouette. We realized that every minute it was gulping down the food supply for thousands of people.

"This is the end of the world," I said.

July 3

Baa-aah! There they are. I can't really see them, but they seem to spend most of their time over in the copse. The sheep. Sheep, plural and singular in the same word. I think of the critic Horace Engdahl. Several years ago I admired—or at least, I was interested in—him and others like him. Someone said he seemed worried about ending up alone and insignificant. He who is afraid of being alone has perhaps never had true company, he who is afraid of insignificance . . . Bah.

July 5

The ewes are lying there neatly by the garden. The group doesn't look that big. There should be twelve, plus sixteen lambs, but closer up it looks more like . . . nine. They seem content. They like lying on a little slope, looking down. As if they knew what was what.

July 10

Small paths appear across the fields. The sheep follow one another so as not to trample the pasture. I never would have thought of that idea myself.

July 13

It's hot. They lie in the shade under the great oaks. In spite of their wool, it's said they don't suffer from the heat. Sheep were historically desert animals. There is an old so-called pasture pump in the field. The animals can pump water up themselves from a well. There's a kind of lid over the water trough, and when it's kicked away the pump mechanism starts. It's actually made for cows, and of the sheep, only one of the older ewes ever manages to bring up any water—and only when she gets cross. I walk over and pump up a few liters. They don't actually drink that much.

August 1

You have to check the sheep at least once a day. In the summer they get along fine by themselves, so it's mostly a case of checking they're still alive and that there's water. There are a few of us on the farm who try to look after the sheep collaboratively. We've had various systems for dividing up the duties, people have come and gone, but the sheep have remained. One system was based on us writing down times. "One check on the field, ten minutes." In hindsight it seems unworkable. It took the charm away a little too. One of the fun things about keeping sheep is that now and then it feels like something other than a job or a duty. Perhaps the feeling can best be summed up by the idea that it's not I who keep the sheep, but the sheep who keep me.

August 11

I wander out into the field. All fine. A ewe is standing a little off from the others. She looks at me, then looks into the distance and bleats. Why I don't know. She probably doesn't either.

August 18

We have a separate group of ram lambs. The reason being that they are starting to reach sexual maturity and so might try to mate with the ewes. Sheep puberty seems, however, to have another effect—the rams become more and more set on escaping. They've got out of the field almost every day these last few weeks, and recently it's escalated. It feels as though they run away as soon as my back is turned. I have to find out how they do it. Today I was hovering about near the flock, trying not to draw attention to myself. Pretty soon I saw how two or three of them were taking the initiative and jumping over the fence. A spontaneous solution was just to grab them by the horns and drag them into the round barn. They can stew on their sins there for a couple of days. We keep a little extra hay in the barn. The result was that the rest of the ram lambs stopped escaping, at least for the time being.

August 19

Today the sheep were in good spirits. I began by moving one of the runaway rams in the barn back into the meadow, to see if he'd learned his lesson. He snuck out straightaway. I carried him into the barn again and took out another. He stayed with the flock. The two left in the barn will probably never stop escaping, and we can't waste winter feed. They'll have to be slaughtered.

August 20

I went out to the savages in the barn. They looked at me contrarily. You're going to be slaughtered, I thought. They got some hay. Then I looked in on the others. There's a lot of thistles in the forest pasture. I lured the rams out with pellet feed. They'll soon learn to follow the bucket, it'll be easier to move them then. Then I tinkered with the little field closest to the barn. Just a bit of everyday maintenance, rather than improvements as such. Like being middle-aged, going sideways forward. Opened the gate to the forest pasture so the ewes can wander into both.

August 23

Now the ewes are escaping too. They got out this morning. But at least it was easy to get them in again. You know where they went out, and if you herd them ahead of you, they go back to the hole in the fence. It's as though they actually want to be home in the field, but they don't quite know how to contain themselves when they see an opening. I felt a twinge of recognition. I guess it's only . . . human?

August 24

Today the ewes went back nicely, this time through a smaller hole. I tried to get the electric fencing we put up inside the sheep mesh to work in the forest pasture, but it wasn't brilliant. I moved them to Sam's field and turned the electricity on there. That worked better. The first year we had sheep there was a guy who came to the farm who taught some of us how to shear and a few other bits and bobs. We asked if the sheep got used to being sheared from one time to the next, but he said sheep only had three things on their minds: eating, bonking, and holes in fences, they take everything else as it comes. All the ewes had found the same tiny, tiny hole and what's more, they went back the same way.

August 25

Maybe the sheep escape because they instinctively want to move between different areas. A flock should ideally be moved between different folds on a pasture. The pasture is better utilized, because none of the grass is allowed to grow too high. According to one old saying, sheep shouldn't hear the church bells ringing in the day of rest more than once before they're moved.

August 28

One of the newcomers to the farm has become interested in the sheep. She wrote this in our messenging group: "The leader of the rams ate peas out of my hand and snuffled in my face. Don't want to slaughter him, can he be a mating ram?" I replied: "I knew this would happen! You've developed real feelings for them. In sheep-rearing, as in life, feelings cause problems. Also, we shouldn't use the ewe's sons or nephews for mating. The offspring will be cross-eyed and have low IQs. Even lower I mean." Earlier in the same conversation she wrote (and this is really something): "Today things came full circle for the savages. We prepped with a glass of blueberry wine each, then fetched them from the food cellar and butchered them in the cider-pressing room. We got two prime fillets, eight steaks, four racks, and the offcuts to be ground for mince. I cooked the fillets for dinner later. Massaged smashed rosemary and garlic into them lovingly. It was one of the best things I've ever eaten. A kind of religious experience."

August 30

Today I've done almost nothing with the little woolly ones. But I think of them. I checked the ewes' water. Even walked up and stood among the flock, to get them used to human contact. Trust has a tendency to erode, in life as in the sheep biz.

August 31

New message: "I'm lying here, listening to the sheep, they bellow, they walk about below my room. Why are they making that noise? Chose knives from the catalogue yesterday. Ordering today." Love and bloodlust in the same breath.

September 4

Another uneventful day among the sheep. I look in on
them and begin to think of other things. A little like
Brokeback Mountain.

September 5

I'm beginning to understand something of the psychology of agriculture. For instance, I don't think as much about the weather or other colors or qualities in the landscape as aesthetic. It's like, there's no bad or good weather, there's just practical circumstances. Crisp and clear—check the water hasn't frozen. Windy—make sure the big door is fixed to the wall. Rainy—wear something sensible.

Leaves turning—maybe time for winter feed. But I guess there's a beauty inherent in all this.

September 9

Today the ewes met me in the yard. Lovely, but a bit inappropriate. I herded them back in and made the fence better.

September 15

I'm sick. If the sheep had escaped today, they would have had the run of the farm. Checked the water.

September 17

I was actually in bed all day yesterday. My wife said I needed to recuperate. But I snuck out and repaired a bit of the fence so it's fixed between the barn and the gate. I tried to move the rams without success and gave the ewes some water.

September 21

This virus just won't pass. The rams won't follow the bucket. I haven't the strength to extend the fence, which needs to be finished before the ewes go into the barn. At least they got some water. And then there was a hole in the garden enclosure that needed mending.

September 22

I have pneumonia. I've only seen the ewes from a distance. And I'm praying for the rams.

September 26

Back on my feet, more or less. Looked in on the rams this morning. They're well. The ewes too. The rams have a salt lick, the ewes need a new one.

October 3

Checked the rams and wedged open the door to the barn where the water trough is. I moved the ewes to the garden field. The gate to the forest enclosure is open too. There's a lot of clover in the corner facing the yard, I hope the little ewes fatten themselves up a little.

September 27

The pasture's getting worse. This is the point at which it would be good to have a decent pasture rotation. If I'd managed to move the ewes between the different folds regularly throughout the summer, there would have been more to eat.

There's a plan for that. I've divided up the fields. Behind the shed there's two hectares of good pasture, split into three different folds. Then we have a few small fields around the yard and in the copse by the road, which make up another two hectares together. But there's been no order to the rotation. It's mostly been about finding the fold where the fence is holding together at that particular moment. There's a rule of thumb for the amount of pastureland required, like five ewes per hectare. I can't remember, I don't think that's quite right either. For now we've got enough, that much I do know.

October 1

Without the aid of machines and fossil fuels it would be really hard to keep sheep. Maybe it wouldn't even be possible. Although if (when) fossil fuels run out, the sheep will probably manage better than the shepherd. For a long time I've been trying to fix in some fence posts. It's a little stretch across stony, hard ground. Macadam was probably laid there at some point to provide better grip for tractor wheels. The sheep seem to love escaping just here, and the posts are all wonky. It's been impossible to get the posts down more than about ten inches, but today it suddenly worked. I got the tractor and drove the forks into the ground. They left deep holes and the posts set like stone.

October 2

I finished the fence by the shed, and yelled a few times like Astrid Lindgren's fearsome Ronja. It was so great to be finished. I hope none of the real farmers heard me. I hope no one heard me. Or actually, I hope the sheep did hear me. They probably need something to think about. They're doing fine and all, but it must be a bit boring to just trudge around. Just imagine only having your basic needs to concern you. Am I hungry, thirsty? Am I cold? You'd be going crazy. Or completely at peace.

October 10

I had a Spaniard with me in the field today. He talked the whole time, the ewes looked at him sternly. Then I screwed up a winch in the abattoir.

October 11

The shearing this morning went well. It's almost the first time I felt like I had full control over the process. It has taken time and cost a lot of blood, sweat, and tears. But it's been worth it. The blood has mostly come from the ewes, but today I did almost no damage.

October 19

The ewes are well. They snuck out and took a turn in the autumn-sown wheat. I let them amuse themselves for a while as I mended the fence. Fresh wheat sprouts are meant to be good for them. Last year I asked the farmer who uses the field whether the sheep's antics and their grazing on the delicate shoots affected the harvest. "Not at all," he replied with a wry smile.

November 2

The ewes awoke (if they even slept) to snow-covered pasture. They were in the barn. I opened it yesterday and put out a little hay. Most of the winter feed is made up of silage that we buy from the real farmers, but we take some in ourselves. We scythe the grass and put it up in what could generously be called a haystack. A lot of work, little fodder, but not everything we do in this life can be one hundred percent rational. In any case, it's a special feeling to give this little clump of hay to the sheep just when the first snow has settled. It's like saying: "We took this in many months ago and saved it for exactly this kind of occasion, when it's cold and windy and snowy and the grass in the field is all gone. You couldn't have done that yourselves." I don't know if it's gratitude in the sheep's eyes, perhaps a sort of simplified form of wonder: "Aha, we were thinking we'd just lay down here and die, but look here's some hay."

November 3

I messaged the others: "Looked at rams today, Gute. Good size, nice colors, horns. I like them. Choosing between Affe and Brolle. Both pale, a little stripey. Thoughts? Almost time for tupping. This week ideally. For the sheep I mean."

November 5

We went with Brolle. He was with an elderly couple
about twelve miles away. They have ten to fifteen ewes.
Small-time sheep-owners have a tendency to give their
rams somewhat over-the-top names. One we bought
from named them after famous feminists. For a while
we were looking at Claes Borgström, but decided on
The Phantom (he protects women, apparently). Brolle's
farmers were nice. She showed me photos of her grand-
children, he showed me pictures of the sheep. We went
over each of our families and circles of acquaintance
with a fine-tooth comb to get a complete survey of all the
links we had in common. There was something about
my aunt, I didn't quite get it. That's how it works in the
country, like Facebook, except you can never log out.
We got Brolle into the trunk. Once he was in the field
with the ewes, he got the idea straightaway. A bit of nos-
ing about and then off he went. Is this really natural?

November 15

Today I've spent quite a lot of time getting the on-farm register in shape. Everything has to be in order now it's almost time for testing for MV accreditation. It turns out that two of the sheep have the same number, 006. It doesn't mean that much I guess, we can tell them apart easily, one is gray and one is a little grayer. But how has it happened? I can believe a lot of them, but not that they give each other ear tags.

November 16

For a while I thought the sheep didn't like our silage, but today they ate hungrily and with great focus. It turns out they got into the garden for a while yesterday. A post in the newly renovated part of the fence had fallen down. The post seems to want to lift itself out of the hole in the ground. I hammered in a stone in an attempt to wedge it tight. We'll see. A real farmer would have . . . If only I knew what a real farmer would have done.

November 18

Some people think it's lonely to live in the country. I have the sheep. Whether a situation is social or not social probably doesn't depend so much on the exact number of encounters. It has to do with the character of the people you encounter: if you want to identify with them, if they want to identify with you, if you can see yourself reflected in them. There's not so much difference between country and city where social life is concerned. Though here I have the sheep.

November 20

I stand at the big door watching. The snow has gone again, it's still a little green out there. I realize we have a good system here, without us actually planning it from the outset. The barn where the sheep go in and are housed in the winter is adjacent to the largest field. The door is almost always open, meaning they can decide for themselves whether they want to eat more of the winter feed. It's elegant; I mean, who knows better when the grazing is bad in the field than the sheep themselves?

November 24

I turned off the water in one of the summer pastures this morning so the pump won't freeze and burst. I must remember to do the same on the slope and over by the round barn before the temperature drops below zero.

December 2

Sometimes, like today for example, it's almost impossible to get the silage out of the bale. The grass seems to bind to itself. I tug at it, getting sweaty. And angry. We have an idea about working collectively here on the farm, though apparently it doesn't apply to everyone. I'm the only one who does any work, I think crossly. Normally I don't get annoyed, but when I'm working so hard I get short of breath, an unexpected rage bubbles up. It's cleansing.

December 12

There's been less contact with the sheep lately. I go to the round barn, kick at the silage a little, look out through the doors. They're generally out, looking for pasture to graze. They shouldn't be finding anything this late in the year, but the last clumps from the bale are going slowly. I wonder if more bleating when they see me means they want more food. I mean, of course they can't process all the stages in the thought I—want—more—food—give—it—to—me. But perhaps an instinct to communicate with humans has been passed down through the centuries. They are bleating more now. I leave the light on at night, so they can go in when it's dark outside and just nibble on the last bits of silage without thinking about it.

December 13

New silage bale. The first one lasted for almost three weeks. There was a bit of hassle with the tractor before-hand. I changed the radiator myself. It's good to learn, I thought. But I'll probably forget by the next time the radiator breaks. When I put out the bale, I managed to dent the stall railings, so they'll need repairing eventually. Not a big deal, but it feels like we need a new system, more suited to our small scale. Small bales for instance. One of my children was there, getting to know Brolle. The sheep have become a bit less tame this last week. You can see pretty quickly that I've mostly been watching them from a distance instead of taking the time to go into the field.

December 16

Some new sheep mesh arrived by truck the other day.
Felt kind of tempted to repair some fencing.

December 17

Short visit to the sheep today. I was in the round barn, rattling about. They trotted toward me, bleating absent-mindedly. I walked over and prodded around in the silage so they could get to it better. They looked at me skepti-cally; I thought: We have a relationship. They've stopped going to Sam's field, but they're out in the forest pasture fairly often. I wonder if it's mostly from habit that they go and graze, or if they actually prefer frostbitten blades of grass to silage. One seems a bit off. Moving slowly, but she doesn't seem to be in pain at all. Depression?

December 18

I spoke to the vet. She said I could wait but that the ewe should be slaughtered and destroyed if she had a fever and didn't get better. I'm about to check her temperature now.

December 18 (evening)

She's only 103, which is apparently normal for sheep.
She's eating hay and pellet feed, but she's just lying there.
I can't quite believe she's going to survive. We'll see.

December 20

New bale. It was quicker this time. Good technique with the tractor. Bashed the railing again. It creaked a bit, but it was OK. Brolle is often out in front. I don't think he's a leader. He's just the stupidest, the one the others send over when they're unsure what's going on. The ram's mind is fascinating, or perhaps it would be better to say that the meeting of the ram's and the human's minds is fascinating. When they're alone in a flock with ewes, as Brolle is now, the ram is always the one to come forward first, coming up and sniffing around; he brings up the rear, close to the shepherd, when you're driving the flock in front of you; and he loves being scratched on the back and on his throat. It's easy to develop a close relationship, muck around playing with him, get him to walk alongside you and even to come when you call him. A ram can, with a little patience, become just like a dog. For a while, that is. Countless are the stories about people with small flocks getting close to their rams, talking about them like members of the family, before one day deciding with regret that they have to be sold or slaughtered. There's always a turning point at which the ram can no longer handle the intimacy, and they start butting. Someone said this was because rams can't really distinguish between friendship and rivalry, as though it's the same thing in some way. I experienced this with our first ram, The Phantom. We used to cuddle like newlyweds, until one day he gave me a butt on the thigh, hard and emphatic. I was given some bad advice, that I should overpower him and lay him on his back so he would know his place. Once you understand how things work, it's clear that in the long run a ram can only recognize two modes of existence—king of the hill or pushover. The Phantom seemed to accept his place as my obedient friend. Then he butted me again. I got him on his back again. After three days I got rammed again. I tried the same procedure and it worked—for thirty seconds. It was over. We weren't friends anymore. I stayed away. Tending the flock became difficult. It sounds awful, but it was a relief when we slaughtered him. And it's as though there's something—evolution, the sheep

gods, coincidence or some other supernatural force—
that made it that way. If rams didn't make themselves
impossible to deal with after a while, we would never be
able to slaughter them and then we wouldn't have taken
such good care of them from the start.

December 22

The sick ewe seems to be recovering. She's grazing with the others. Her name is 195. It might seem a little impersonal, using numbers, but it still feels adequate. The sheep are a flock first and foremost, not individuals. We only give real names to the mating rams. It's not because we respect them more, but because they have an individual task for the time being.

December 28

Now the shepherd's old winter routines are starting again. It's the same every year. The water freezes. I take the kettle down. Unfortunately I couldn't get the water going today. It's minus twenty and the water in the pipe has frozen. I'll have to put a tub out this evening. Maybe it's time for a new bale of straw too.

January 6

New hay bale in the stall. It's for lying on and eating too. Straw is junk food I think. I was getting rid of some old fencing, and at the same time I got a little lecture from the real farmer with cows, on all the parameters that have to be taken into account when harvesting hay. He has dairy cows and needs there to be as much energy as possible in the feed. Our "production" takes place mainly during summer while the lambs are growing, with only natural grazing as feed.

During the winter the ewes are in lamb, and perhaps we should pay more attention to the winter feed. We are happy if they're full. It's tricky to read up on what you should do, because the decisions depend on whether you want to maximize productivity or do everything as cheaply as possible. There's no right or wrong, you have to make up your own mind. So, a new silage bale it was. The last one only lasted ten days, but it took the sheep through the worst cold spell and they had no straw to munch on alongside.

January 8

Worked on fence yesterday. It's not really the right time of year, we're on the wrong chapter of the farming guide, so to speak. But we're not that traditional in the first place. The sheep were scared of the roll of sheep mesh. They looked at it nervously and tried to get as far away from it as possible. The new silage is totally different, moist and probably richer in energy. They eat it hungrily. I fixed the saw too, the one you saw the posts into points with. There's a few things to be getting on with. I also hooked up the electricity in the little bit of fencing where we're trying just electric fence and no sheep mesh. Works perfectly. Quite a lot of fuss to hook up the unit in the white barn, but it feels like a good solution in the long term.

January 12

They're eating the feed that seems higher in protein, but seem to be leaving the straw. Now the snow is settling, which makes work on the fence tough. I put the rest of the roll of mesh by the gable of the red barn. The stretch over toward the greenhouse will be the next project. Parts of a big oak blew down up by the croft near the forest. That'll make a lot of nice stakes.

January 15

It occurred to me to check on the condition of some of the ewes today. The completely white mixed-breeds are good and fat, you hardly feel any bones when you feel over their hips. Brolle was a little frailer, and 195 was properly thin. Not good, but better than culling and destroying her. I'll gradually try to check them all. Perhaps we can give them individual supplementary feed. It was easy to do that when 195 was on her own in the barn and the others were outdoors, but if I put in pellet feed now the strongest ones would just eat it all.

January 16

Felt a few more of the ewes. The Helsinge sheep are a little skinnier than the mixed-breeds. We've got proper lighting sorted in the round barn now. A boost, for me and the sheep. I didn't go over there until five in the afternoon. It was dark outside and not all of them were in. I only saw nineteen, there should be twenty-two.

January 17

Felt a few more ewes. They were nice and fat.

January 18

New bale. They seemed hungry and were standing waiting by the rack where the bales go. I got it in place without incident. Key concepts: Take your time, learn from your experiences, do the same thing continually and consistently. In other words: be a farmer. Or just do things properly.

January 26

The sheep seem to enjoy the snow. They stay close to the barn, but they're as happy out as in. Once or twice I've seen them heading for the forest. They come into the barn when I'm there. I think they pull out the best of the silage, so when I come over and put out some new stuff they all want to be there first. A couple of ewes are always right at the back of the flock and seem to get to the feed last. I thought there would be enough space for all twenty of them to eat at the same time, but it's like they don't let each other through. Five of them can block almost the whole manger.

February 1

Now I think I've checked the condition of all of them.
Four or five are maybe a bit skinny, one of them is 195.
I'll check again in two weeks, if things stay the same we'll
have to help them somehow.

February 2

I wonder how it is for the owners of other kinds of animals. I don't develop such strong ties to individuals as for instance dog owners do, but on the other hand, I'm tied to the whole apparatus of keeping sheep. I don't make appointments or plan to get various things done—I just do it. Keeping sheep demands a presence and a continuity that makes it more than a hobby. I am forced, regardless of the time of year, to tend the sheep in some way every day, and in practice, take care of them round the clock. It's a big commitment, and you're not really sure what you get in return. Meat? Wool? It's more the commitment that's the reward. You don't need to think about whether you have enough to do in your life, because what you have to do is standing two hundred yards away in a field ruminating, completely—I mean really totally and utterly—oblivious to such distinctions.

February 6

I have a little treasure trove of old bits of pipe. No real plumber would even look at this junk, but for me it often solves problems. I never have exactly the bit I need, so instead I play around with what I have. The sheep's trough is leaking, a joint has to be replaced. I don't have one, so instead I take a strange bent piece of pipe that looks like it came from a restaurant kitchen. That'll do.

February 9

I'm reading about climate change and the worsening outlook for life on earth. Just imagine if this is the end? Maybe the sheep worry about this too. I think a life with sheep is sustainable. In the olden days people only needed sheep. They could be food, warmth, clothing, toys. Now we buy almost everything from China.

February 11

I haven't been doing much with the sheep. I've been doing a fair bit of brooding instead. Last year I shut them up in the barn completely for the last few weeks of winter before the pasture got going, so they wouldn't wear out the grass.

Housing them, it's called. This year I don't know.

February 16

On Saturday I checked their condition again. The four frail ones have put on weight. It was only 195 that was thin as a rake. Their improvement could be down to a number of things. Maybe it's because of the bales and the last two being more protein-rich, maybe it's made a difference that I've been spreading out the feed better and putting out a clump in the middle of the stall every day. That means no one has to stand back and wait to be able to eat.

February 17

I worked for a while under the roof in the barn, and I looked down at the flock from above. They nudge each other a bit by the feed. Brolle and a ewe were butting each other. They're easy to deal with. I don't need to wonder how to get along with them, or what drives them. They don't need pep talks or motivational development powwows. They hardly do anything, unless rumination can be called an occupation.

March 2

They're suddenly eating a lot. The kids played with them a bit. The sheep broke out twice yesterday. Well, "broke out" sounds a bit over the top. They just stood there, staring, and didn't seem to be anywhere. The first time a border collie herded them in, without any particular instructions. It just did it, without seeming to ask why. The second time I herded them back myself, somewhat irresolutely, nervously, where did they get out? Now the fence needs repairing. . . .

March 5

I've been thinking about our relationship with sheep. In a way there's not much going on with them. We stand and stare at each other for a few minutes every day. But taking care of living creatures is about more than relating to individuals. They are in my care, and this is only partially apparent in the mutual staring. Most of the caring is done without the recipients' involvement—the fence, the winter feed, the mucking out, the water. Sheep have been domesticated for eleven thousand years, they say. We look at each other, the sheep and I, and it's like we look down into a deep well of experiences, problems, possibilities, worries, sources of joy—life in all its dimensions and inconceivable scope across time and space.

March 10

Hooves need seeing to. There's a fair bit of literature on the subject. That's no exaggeration. There's so much online and in books about how sheep's feet should be trimmed. Hoof-care is, however, a perfect example of what academics call tacit knowledge (dissertations have been written about it). I'm not sure why this knowledge is tacit, perhaps it's really just unassuming. If you know it, you just do it; if you don't, you have no idea. To be honest, trimming the external parts of the sheep's hooves isn't hard. The difficulty in explaining exactly how it works probably stems from the fact that you need to be holding an actual hoof when you learn. All these books, sites, and theses are like great neurotic compensations for the lack of physical contact. Another key to the skill is mistakes. I think I've slithered around in the ditches on both sides of hoof trimming. One is not trimming at all. I noticed, a few weeks into summer, that a few of the ewes were limping a little. Their hooves were seriously overgrown. Not nice, but at least now I know why they need trimming. The other mistake was to cut too much off. One time, half a hoof pad went along for the ride. The poor sheep bled and limped, but it was OK in the end, and now I know exactly where the line between hoof and pad is.

April 10

A couple of the mums—we call them mums when they've
just had lambs—have been nudging their lambs out of
the way so they can't suckle. We have to hold the mum
still several times a day. To begin with I was really angry
with them, but now I've come to accept that they're just
sheep. You can't identify with these animals. They are
totally different to us.

April 12

Standing in the field, watching. A ewe has just lambed. We've decided to let them lamb out in the field. They can choose their own spot that way. In the barn it gets cramped and unhygienic. They manage all on their own. Some lambs die, that's nature's way, but so far, no ewe has had problems with the actual lambing. She's licking one of the lambs fiercely, the other lies a little way off. (Our sheep almost always have two lambs.) I think to myself that it's a critical moment, this might be the point when she rejects one of the lambs. Soon, I'll carry the lambs into a separate stall in the barn, where there's clean straw and limited space. That way the lambs won't have to walk a long way after the ewe. But I don't want to lift them too soon—the ewe might get the idea the lambs aren't hers. You have to be present, but not overbearing.

April 15

The kids aren't that interested in the challenges of winter feeding and all that, but when the lambs come along, they can't get enough. Then there's hustle and bustle and discussions about who's going to feed the skinny ones and what their names are going to be. Those names will disappear soon enough. At some point in late summer they don't look like lambs anymore. They've become sheep. The rams go to the slaughter, and some of the ewes are allowed to survive, to grow the flock. By that point the kids have forgotten both the names and the sheep. That's the way things are.

April 17

We tried a slightly odd technique to get a ewe to accept a rejected lamb. She was letting one suckle, but shoved the other away. We shut the ewe in a small space and lifted out the lamb she liked. Maybe she'd take to the other now the first one was missing. Now everyone felt sorry for the first lamb. I took it into the house. My daughter put a nappy on it and had it in her bed. Superficially it was pretty cute, but probably a nightmare for the lamb. I took it back after an hour.

May 7

The lambing has gone badly. Almost one in three lambs were much too weak when they were born, some of them died. It's been awful. It might have been a virus, perhaps one of the silage bales was bad, or (terrible thought) maybe they didn't get enough mineral feed. If that's the case, it's my fault—not bad luck, not nature's way—just my fault. The lambing period lasts for about a month; now it's drawing to a close I'm starting to emerge from some sort of stress-related depression. It's not only the sad—perhaps even tragic—fact of lambs dying, it's also been a lot of work, with many lambs needing supplementary feeding with the bottle, and help getting over to the mum.

May 16

A little cold spell is upon us. Last night it was only a couple of degrees above freezing, and it rained. I went out at midnight. There's just one lamb needing help with extra feeding now. With my forehead lamp, into the flock, they're at ease with me, just standing, staring. Where was the little one? Not with its mum, I could see the number tag in her ear. I walked right around the flock, no little white one. Worried. I was humming a pop song. It started to seem like the silly words about love were about me and the lamb. "Where are you? I need you. I never knew I could miss you so much. Can we turn back time? Time is a river.

"Hold back the river, let me look in your eyes, hold back the river so I can stop for a minute and be by your side." There it is, lying there. Blood runs from its throat. A scavenger bird must have already got there.

June 1

The sheep seem to be defined by the flock. Their individual traits are determined by their role in the group. For example, it's almost always the same individual who finds holes in the fence. Some have a greater tendency to defend themselves and the flock, while others stay in the middle, always protected by others. I think they also have slightly different roles in searching for pasture to graze: some seem to get sent out on recon a way off from the group. It's almost as though you can view the flock as a single organism, and the individuals as mere aspects of the same thing. What if sheep view us the same way?

June 14

I meet more people than I need or want to, it's bordering on hectic at times. So the moments with the sheep, particularly when I'm alone, become oases of stillness, contemplation, and dignity. Even when I'm rushing around a flock, trying to get them to jump back over a fence, or overpowering a large ram so I can shear his fur, there's a sublime peace to existence. I think it's because I'm in direct contact with something that is alive but almost unyielding in its own movements. The behavior and habits of the sheep—passed down through endless generations—the grass growing, rain, drought, cold, warmth, food, shit—everything lives its life with no regard for what I think about it. The shepherd is alone, but is in the company of everything.

July 4

We had a Facebook page for a while, to show we existed and let people know what we do on the farm. We grow vegetables for our own consumption, chop wood, keep a few animals and try, without exaggerating or taking it all too seriously (moderation is a virtue), to develop a sustainable way of living. As representative for the sheep-keeping, or for the sheep themselves, perhaps, I posted the following little note: "The sheep don't graze on all the grass in the fields, they choose some blades and leave others. They don't just chomp it all down obliviously. In this way, regrowth is encouraged. In the long term, perhaps over the course of several years, the pasture, and correspondingly, the sheep's life, improves. Thanks to their restraint. A species that constantly satisfies its short-term needs without stopping to think will probably fail." Under the text was a picture of how the landscape is being changed by oil sand extraction in Canada. A flourishing green landscape of forest, lake, and meadow is transformed into a black gravel desert. I thought it was an impactful and singularly striking little reflection. However, it produced only a few stray likes and no comments.

They say social media gives people affirmation. Apparently that doesn't apply to me or the sheep, unless we're lying on a grassy slope in the morning mist, ruminating and acting as if nothing's doing, as if nothing has anything to do with anything else. Perhaps you have to adapt to be liked, but then what kind of love is that?

August 8

A ewe is limping. Sometimes it's just a little stone that's got caught between their toes. I get hold of her and have a look. Can't find anything—no stone, no swelling. I ring the vet. Same as usual: wait and see or cull. But isn't it horrible, limping on one foot? They have four of them, the vet says.

August 20

Someone asked what the sheep smell of. I don't really know, I've never thought about it. It's probably in the . . . nose of the beholder. The ewes have a gland right next to their teats. It looks like a suppurating wound and it really puts you off trying to find out what it smells like. The gland guides the newborn lamb, presumably with scent. My family tend to say I smell of sheep when I've been shearing them. I think the smell is like that of a well-worn sweater: bearable, but still time for a wash.

September 1

Walking behind the flock. They're almost jogging ahead of me. What happened to the one who was limping actually? I can't even remember what she was called. I chase the flock a little more to check none of them has any problems. The ones with ailments always fall behind. Not a rock solid system, but it'll have to do.

October 17

Screwed in the gates ahead of the slaughter. It went badly. I mishit and split a bolt. I'll have to buy a new one. But I won't give up.

October 19

It's impossible to describe the slaughter. Perhaps because it's repulsive, perhaps because the borderline between life and death simply can't be apprehended.

You're either alive or you're not. In between, emptiness, nothing, antimatter. It's like a vertical drop at a theme park. Your whole body is screaming no, all your reactions are in revolt, but you're resolved. You will see it through. And it's fine. But there's no euphoria or relief afterward. Rather a deep gray sense of completion. No year with the sheep is complete before the slaughter is finished; life with the sheep can't come full circle until it's done.

October 21

Extended the fence yesterday from the field to the abattoir. Actual time spent: 1.5 hours. Still it feels like it took the whole day.

October 22

I've got my hands on a bolt gun. The man who lived in one of the houses on the farm before we moved here had one. "You can have it," he said, "I never use it." I asked what caliber it was. "No, no," he said, "it's not for amateurs." The batteries in his hearing aid must have run out again.

October 24

A few thoughts the day after the slaughter. It's the first year we've done everything ourselves. Previously we've got a professional in, a nice fellow who used to work at the meat production company Scan, but now he's a caregiver—in mental health, I think. We've been able to look away or pretend we weren't really involved. Now we're right in the middle of it all. There's a lot of blood and death and you don't get inured. Twelve dead sheep are twelve dead sheep. Twelve shots with the bolt gun are twelve crushed skulls. Nothing less. There's an old tradition of drinking shots before the slaughter. I realize now it's not for the fun of it.

October 30

I check the skins. We salted them right after the slaughter. After a week or so, you're supposed to check on them to see whether they need more salt. The fat mustn't be allowed to go rancid. The real slaughterman was really good at skinning; it's a tricky task. It's easy to accidentally make holes. You can't really see how well we've done. We'll see when we get to the tannery.

November 18

I can't stop thinking about what I'm doing. And think again and then start all over again. Dwell on things, many would say. Like this—writing down the detail of my days with the sheep. How should it sound? Quite a big part of the work is solitary and rather boring, gray, and uneventful. Should my notes also be a little dull?

November 22

Check on the sheep, wet, cold, windy.

November 22 (evening)

Tightened a connection for the water, which is leaking,
cold . . . wet.

November 23

Scooping up silage, it's wet, heavy.

November 24

Check on the sheep, no change.

November 25

Silage, wet.

November 26

Check, nothing to see.

November 27

Is 264 limping?

November 28

No.

November 29

I think?

January 5

I flick through my notes. It strikes me that my existence here has become something completely different to what I had anticipated. That I would bond so strongly, not just to the sheep themselves, but to the fields, the weather's quirks, the character of the seasons, the grass, the trees, the bushes, the barns, the fences, the planks, the nails, everything—I didn't believe that. When we moved here, we had ideas about collectives, self-reliance, and living sustainably, or something. It didn't quite turn out how we imagined, especially the collective thing. (Just imagine, the skeptics are always proved right.) For long periods I've been alone with the sheep. At first I was cross, not so much at the people who weren't present, but that normal life had such a strong pull. Having a job, taking off whenever, doing conventional things—all this turned out to be easier than looking after the sheep. And I understand that; it's not as though our lives hinge on keeping sheep, exactly. There's nothing tangible that would motivate you to be a small-scale (that is to say, unprofitable) sheep farmer, but still, the sheep require a degree of work commitment. The animals can't wait for you to feel like taking care of them, like my aunt once said. Now I've learned not to care about trying to motivate others—learned not to care what kinds of hopes and expectations they have. I take care of the sheep and am satisfied. We've gone through disappointments together, the sheep and I. It forms a bond. Not to the individuals, they're slaughtered sooner or later, but to the flock and its needs. I'm not cross with anyone anymore.

February 15

I've begun to read books again. Why, I don't know. Maybe because the sheep don't escape anymore. The difference is probably that the electric fence is in better order. The winter routines are also going much more smoothly. The water almost never freezes. For a while I seemed to spend all my time fixing that system—there's an element in the water pipe that keeps the temperature up—but now it seems to work as long as you like. What if there's a final fix, one that will work forever? The feed racks have also stopped breaking. I can hardly complain at this development, but now I'm sitting inside, gazing at the bookshelves. During those first years here on the farm, the books sank into the background. They became part of the furniture, like a tasteful interruption to the wallpaper. I quickly find my way back to the old tracks. Roland Barthes: "I conclude that in order to correct my message (that is, in order for it to be exact), I must not only vary it, but also that this variation must be original and apparently invented." He's talking about literature.

I think about how it might apply to everything, that, in order for something to be genuine, for real, you have to avoid routine, experience, even knowledge. When you get too good at things it's not fun anymore. It's hard to make the same joke twice in a row. I hope the sheep retain their inscrutability. Maybe they'll outwit the electricity.

March 10

As a small farmer, you become more and more sensitive to details and signals. On the brink of spring, in the transition from winter feed to grazing, you have to judge whether the sheep are hungry, if the grazing is enough or you need to put out a new silage bale. It seems easy when you know how, but it's taken some years to get to that point. When I walk in among the flock, I notice how hungry they are from how much they bleat, and whether they make their way toward me.

Sometimes they even go up to the gate leading to the next field in the rotation. It's perhaps not just so much that I'm now able to read their signals, but also that the sheep have learned to give these signals. We have each other, the sheep and I.

April 3

They don't just eat grass, hay, and silage, they really live with it. Straw gets caught in their wool, they get grass stains on their knees. If I didn't know better I could well imagine that they took in the vegetable fibers through their ears, eyes, and, yes, even through their skin.

April 12

I saw an advert for some organization for Swedish farmers. There was a man sitting at sunrise, looking out across his fields, quite large, flat fields, plowed with a reversible plow. He climbs into his tractor, looking like a passenger in a big bus. The voice-over talks about how the farmer lives off the land and therefore takes care of it. I find it almost impossible to conjure a more screwed-up world. If you know the slightest thing about how the ecosystem works, you'll know that large-scale agriculture is waging a bona fide extinction campaign against large numbers of animal and plant species. What's more, it systematically impoverishes the soil—without the addition of artificial fertilizers, nothing would grow in the long term—and is a monstrous energy drain. Sweden's farmers are skilled and hardworking, but taking care of nature is not something they do. At the same time, we and our sheep are dependent on farmers with big tractors. I dream, a little uncertainly, about bringing in our winter feed by hand, or maybe with the help of horses. Which would then need winter feed too.

April 21

I want to believe we're becoming more professional every year (whatever that's worth). One thing is that we have one, and sometimes two, sheepdogs now. Many tasks that used to descend into total farce are now done in a flash, for example splitting a group into two and moving one of them to a new pasture. Today it was chaos again. We were going to move the ewes and their lambs into a field they'd never been in before. Ewes with lambs have a totally different psychology to regular sheep. It's as though the flight instinct has completely vanished, as has the drive to keep the flock together. They're thinking only of the lambs. They didn't move for the dogs, and some even went on the attack. Pretty soon we put the dogs back up on the trailer again. We tried luring with pellet feed. That didn't work either. In the end we were basically forced to push them along in front of us.

April 22

I think the fox has taken a lamb. The field we moved the sheep up to yesterday is a bit farther away from the farm, up by the edge of the main woodland. One of the lambs still needed supplementary feeding with a bottle and had been partly rejected by its mother. When we got there in the morning with the bottle, it didn't come to us, it was gone. I spoke to one of our neighbors, a hunting nut. He said a fox could take ten to fifteen lambs during the spring, that they have big problems in England, that you have to hunt the fox hard, that he has a friend with a terrier that can "clean out" the den. I concluded our conversation. But I couldn't stop myself sneaking up to the edge of the woods and lying down, waiting with the rifle. I've never shot a fox; I had one in my sights once, but hesitated too long. Hunting's not my thing. I lay there watching for an hour until it was pitch-black. Then I walked over to the sheep. They'd assumed battle formation. Eighteen ewes and thirty-seven lambs were pressed together on an area of around 250 square feet, with the ewes on the outside and the lambs in the middle. They'll probably be all right.

April 30

I've lost that daily contact with the sheep. New people have come to the farm who want to be involved. These last few days, someone else has been checking in on them, counting the lambs, seeing how much they've been growing, seeing where they're grazing, which stones they're jumping up onto, taking stock of the atmosphere in the group. It feels empty. It's easy to think it's a bit irritating to be bound by your duty to the animals, that it's stressful to feel you have to be there every day, that you're not totally free. In fact, it's just the opposite. I sit in the kitchen staring into space. There's nothing free about that.

May 2

I'm not a vain person, but when I've been shearing sheep it's as though I've wanted to be seen. Every time the sheep shearing has come around, there's been a lot of talk and planning. There are the wool ladies who come by, the neighbours who watch, the children "helping out." It's been as though a little fair has come to town. And I'm not even that good at shearing. This time I just head down to the barn and make a start; no one else is at home on the farm, and suddenly I understand the true meaning of sheep shearing. I understand it in a pretty vague way, but with certainty, and without words. The wool is oily and scratchy.

May 3

The unsustainability of the world makes itself known all the time. Or rather . . . everything is simply unsustainable, all the time. I don't really understand why everyone acts as if nothing's happening, acts as though we had these great ideas in place that were going to make a difference. I've been learning a bit about forestry, because I inherited a plot of woodland (there's always a reason). Clear-cutting is one of the things contributing to the end of human life on earth. You don't really notice it, it's like a net in which one thread after another wears out and in the end everything suddenly breaks. Using clear-cutting as a forestry technique will, sooner or later, weaken ecological ties and functions so much that they quite simply stop holding together or working any longer. Laudably, the Swedish Forest Agency has put some resources into developing forms of forestry that don't use clear-cutting. If you talk to the people at the Forest Agency, you get the impression that this "alternatives to clearing" stuff is all the rage now, it's happening, lots of people are interested. I asked what kind of area was on the way to being converted. At a generous estimate, it's a matter of a fraction of a percentage point of productive woodland.

May 9

We're enclosing a brand-new field. Or, well, it's been a field for several hundred years, but with barbed wire and cows. We're changing to electric fencing, so the sheep can go in and graze with the cows. The cows belong to the real farmers who lease the land and a barn here. They—the farmers, that is—are nothing but positive toward our alternative way of doing things. When we moved here, I'd been expecting more resistance. But I guess they realize we're never going to take over.

May 11

I wasn't born a farmer, but I am becoming a farmer. Not a farmer as in agriculturalist, producer of agricultural goods or entrepreneur. I'm becoming a farmer in that narrow-minded, antisocial, conceited way. I have the sheep and I don't need anything else. Whatever happens in the world . . . What's happening in the world, actually?

May 13

More animals are coming to the farm. Pigs—fun, sociable, simple, quite like us humans (apart from the fact that
off milk is their favorite food); horses—powerful, loyal,
useful, not at all like us humans (apart from the fact that
they are latently bonkers). But I still have a special feel
for the sheep. There's something still, unpretentious,
and stoical about them that speaks to me. I do a round
of the field. Really I ought to be checking the tension in
the electric cable, but I stand still in the flock and forget
all about it. I slouch home in the dark, reluctantly, as
though deep down I want to stay out there.

May 16

They get by almost completely without help now. I don't need to spend any work time on them at all, at least as long as the fencing stays intact. Before, spring and summer (and even the autumn to some extent) meant a constant search for holes in the fence, for the sheep just as much as for me. Now we've got a better handle on all that. They have a lot of respect for the electric fence, maybe because they don't really understand electricity, but then, who does?

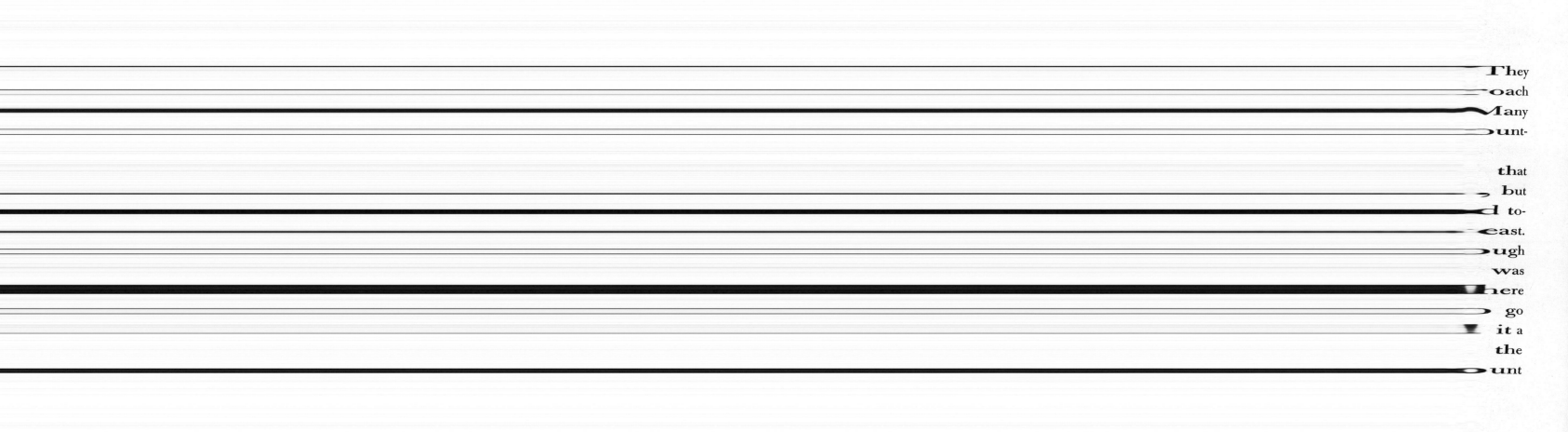

They
oach
Many
ount-

that
but
d to-
east.
ugh
was
here
go
it a
the
unt

June 5

I know what I'm

not even particu

its way through

relationship to t

perhaps I see a l

haps it's precis

half-natural tha

My dad was an

little feet steppe

And perhaps th

my feet. I got an

that can't be ful

who . . . are op

The world fits

with it through

the subjects lai

missed as fanc

during the firs

itself: rational, optimistic about development, urban. It's as though the sheep make me barefoot again. Back to the simple things. But the simple things turn out to be complex, composed of infinite parts.

June 11

I'm reading *H Is for Hawk* by Helen Macdonald. She tames a goshawk and works through the fallout from her father's death. And perhaps her meaningless academic self-image. At first, I don't really understand that this is about acquiring a hunting tool. It's so difficult to imagine that a bird of prey would retain all its competence as a wild animal, while remaining loyal to the owner. I know that's how it was in the past, but it's as though our relationship with the animals here on the farm has made the thought of a tame predator unrealistic. In any case, she describes how she goes out in search of goshawks, and that she gets out of her car like prey from its hiding place. "Something inside me ordered me how and where to step without me knowing much about it. . . . Those old ghostly intuitions that have tied sinew and soul together for millennia had taken over, were doing their thing, making me feel uncomfortable in bright sunlight, uneasy on the wrong side of a ridge, somehow required to walk over the back of a bleached rise of grasses to get to something on the other side: which turned out to be a pond." I can relate.

There's something between me and the sheep that is much older than us, older than these bushes and trees, older than books and knowledge. The bird must learn to jump from its perch to the owner's gloved hand. It doesn't really want to. The hawk just sits there glaring. But then something happens. "My hand is hit, hard, with a blow so unexpectedly powerful the shock is carried down my spine to the tips of my toes. Hitting someone's hand with a baseball bat would have had a similar effect. . . . She has crossed a great psychological gulf, one far wider than the ten inches between her perch and the glove she's landed upon. Not that she's landed on it: she's killed it." This might be a bit of an exaggeration, but I understand that seductive feeling of being in direct contact with nature. I think of a lamb getting a proper grip on the teat for the first time. A tiny little body, barely able to keep itself upright, not to mention orient itself. But when it suddenly gets a good suckle on the teat, the force is almost supernaturally strong. The lamb is immediately much better than me at getting the milk out. When you stand, holding the lamb and the udder, and you feel that unexpected force, it's as though life itself is exerting it.

June 19

We were driving the sheep along the road—that is, the big tarmacked highway outside the farm. It was the long way around, but we, or at least the guy with the dog, wanted to experience that scene when the car has to stop and wait in the midst of a swarm of sheep. And it's fun, everyone thinks so. On this road, no one's in a rush on a Sunday. The sheep don't give a fig for the cars or the tarmac. Sometimes I've fantasized about stopping traffic, as an act of radical resistance to everything that destroys nature. Maybe large numbers of animals on the roads is the method.

June 22

The rams are in the big field up toward the woods. They spread out. You end up taking pretty long walks if you want to count up every one. I don't manage to get to all of them every day.

June 24

My wife flicks through the diary. "What happened to 195 in the end?" she asks. I have precise notes from the lambing somewhere else. 195: Two healthy lambs without comments. And that was during the unhappy spring when many ewes had problems. Nature is unfathomable.

June 25

I'm vegetarian. Though I eat meat from our lambs. Ethics and morals are tricky things. I became vegetarian when I realized what kind of murderous industry was producing the meat in the shops. But I also realized that animals are creatures with nervous systems and feelings. Meat is the remains of dead individuals, parts of corpses. For a while I felt the same resistance to eating animals as to eating people. Then I got sheep. And children. Life is not so simple, I thought then. I began to eat meat again, but only meat that comes from animals I've been involved in killing myself. It's not possible to calculate the best moral position. Well, some people think it is, but there is still always a surplus in all calculations of right and wrong, something left over that you can't really get a grip on. It's like love. It's impossible to exactly and completely describe why you love someone. That wouldn't be love, it would be an investment decision or something similar.

June 26

I'm making some time for the rams. Now I'm going to count them properly, be completely sure the number is correct. Perhaps this kind of grazing land is the most authentic in this area here. The woodland has been cleared and planted in most places, the arable land is plowed and drained. But the grazing fields have probably been the same for many generations. In the middle of the field is an old oak trunk with some kind of iron mounting, could it be two hundred years old? The ground is stony and uneven. You can't grow things in it, but the grass thrives. I come up onto an outcrop, and gaze several miles out over the landscape. If I, purely hypothetically, wanted to show off some of my surroundings, it would be here. Now I've been here for half an hour and the rams are curious. They come up to me, and I can count them all just by standing on a stone.

June 27

We had rather high-minded theories about growing our own food and so on when we started. I grew tired of it after a while. I myself don't need any explanation of why I keep sheep. It comes naturally. Fencing, feed . . . all of that. But people wonder. Like . . . why? Do you kill the animals yourself? Is it hard? Do you have to see to them every day? Isn't it restrictive? I try to say they can join in and do something similar themselves, but mostly they just want me to say something political. I've completely lost the ability to formulate something political in relation to mending sheep mesh or carrying a lamb over to the dry straw by the heat lamp. If I ever possessed it. But you have to be polite. I reply to those who ask. If I wanted to avoid justifying anything in my life, I would need to have a regular job, a regular house, regular friends, and not do anything unexpected. And the funny thing is that a life like that should really raise questions, because you're a participant in and grotesquely rewarded by an economic and political system that, from the ecosystem's perspective, can only be understood as death and extinction, and, for the poorer half of the world's population, as pure apartheid. What's more, some people, perhaps even the majority, have the gall to put limits on how many people from vulnerable and poor parts of the world can come into the country. As though we had some sort of sole right to the surplus bestowed on us by nature.

June 28

There's a little café on the farm now. A few sheepskins hang from one wall, for sale, should anyone want them. I was sitting, drinking coffee, when suddenly someone said: "There's the shepherd himself." "Are these your sheep?" a man asks eagerly. I don't know why I couldn't just answer with a straight-up yes. Perhaps an inherited reaction from generations of shepherds who know that the sheep are only yours in a superficial, all too civilized sense. But OK, if the skins are to be sold, perhaps I'll be the one being paid. We talked about colors, patterns, and woolliness, or rather—he asked questions more quickly than I could answer them, he appeared to know more about it than me. He even proposed a price, but seemed immediately to think it was too much.

June 29

For a period of my life, I thought literature was something special; that words and phrases were tied to and touched our musings, thoughts, and feelings. I thought that a novel, or perhaps just a phrase, could allow a whole world to emerge, strange yet suddenly familiar. These days I think that everything that happens is a kind of poetry. A raven crows over the sheep flock. It's probably saying something. Ravens can grow old, perhaps this one is older than I am, perhaps it's seen the farm change during our years with the sheep. At some point it's surely come down to pick at a dead lamb. The spontaneous literature of this existence needs no one's appreciation or approval, it belongs to no one, neither author nor reader. It lives its own life, letting the words come and go.

June 30

I ring the county administrative board. If the flock grows, we will at some point pass the limit at which you need to register your activities. I find out we have a way to go still, but you still need to follow the rules. Yes, yes. An important point is to put the manure on a concrete surface, so that all the nitrogen doesn't leach out into the ground. I know we have one behind the old barn. Everything works out.

July 2

I've been thinking about meat and about that time I was a proper vegetarian. Perhaps the main reason was that eating meat seemed like something so vulgarly greedy. In our consumer culture, everything is constantly available. There's nothing we need do without. And that's where eating meat became the thing that summarized everything most clearly. To feed up and kill animals on an industrial scale to create a life of luxury and surplus is not right. It might be pathetic and, in particular, misguided to be a vegetarian and still live the same frivolous life, but at least it's something. I moved out to the country and got sheep so I could get away from that hedonistic nightmare. It hasn't really worked. I'm still living in surplus. If the meat in the freezer runs out, I just head to the supermarket. I'll probably be punished for it in future, but I can't figure out any way of escaping it. In secret I hope all the comfort and accessibility, in which a debit card solves all the problems of daily life, will disappear.

If this ground, these pastures, and these sheep were all I had, which has been the reality of human life for the best part of our time on earth, the slaughter and meat-eating would have nothing to do with morality or sustainable lifestyles whatsoever. It would be a way of living, and no more.

Sun, wind, water, earth, organisms, and a little fencing, in an organically interlinked whole, touchable only by God. And hardly even that, actually.

July 4

As I said, I'm turning into a farmer, cross and self-sufficient. But I can't stop thinking about my place in the world. Not because I'm particularly important, but because I, just like everyone else, am part of the greater whole. Something terrible happened in the field a few weeks ago, which illustrated the phenomenon "part of the greater whole." A lamb died, I was forced to shoot it, my children were there. But I don't think the lamb's mum, the ewe, or any others in the flock, or my children, mourned it. I don't say that in order to trivialize something tragic and unpleasant. I just think it's true. What happened was that one of our horses trampled the lamb so badly it had to be put down. We didn't see it happen, but that must have been what occurred. We'd let the sheep into the horses' field a few days earlier, and I saw that the lambs were curious. They'd go up to the horses and nose about until the horses got irritated and chased them away. This lamb must have been the least cautious one; it chased around the horse's leg and got under a hoof. When I got to the field, it lay in a little hollow and couldn't get up. One of its forelegs was bent at an unnatural angle. I tried to stand it up, but it lost its balance straightaway, and just lay there, sprawling. The children were playing with the horses. They saw me and the lamb. "I have to shoot it," I said. When I came back with the rifle, the kids were standing round the lamb. "There's nothing we can do, back off now." I shot the lamb in the back of the head. The kids came over and saw thick blood running from its mouth. A fact of life? I don't know. My daughter went back to the horses, one of my sons helped me to carry the lamb away. We put it in a plastic garbage bag. I would bury it the following day. Without making things too easy for myself, I think it's about learning from our mistakes. For the lamb of course, this wasn't an experience, it was just death and nothing more, but for the flock as a whole it was an important lesson: don't go too near the horses. In this way, the flock doesn't mourn a lost individual, it feels a pain in a part of the collective sheep body. It's a wound that causes pain, but it heals and the flock lives on, stronger and more full of life.

July 23

It's dry. The pastures are drying out. The sheep are bleating. They come up to me when I go out into the field, as though asking *me* for rain.

September 10

The nature in this region is not particularly natural. The more I learn about the woods, the fields, the meadows, the lakes and the rivers and canals, roads and buildings, the more I realize that everything is interwoven with the activity of human beings. And it has been that way for a very long time, it's even difficult to determine what is natural for nature here. Under the layers of civilization you can see now, there are other layers of human activity from previous ages that have formed the surroundings. It's meaningless to try to imagine a natural state here, much less recreate it. I don't think sheep have ever been a big thing here. The ground is too fertile for such a hardy, underproductive animal. And yet there's something historic and natural I sense when I follow the flock, the way they graze, move, search for food in the pastures and in the woods. I think about how their behavior, skills, and character come down to millennia of development. But perhaps time and history are irrelevant. The sheep are what they are, here and now; they just make the best of the situation. The first we got came from Värmland, 200 miles away. Since then we've imported a few rams, also from fairly far away. Neither genetically nor traditionally do they have anything to do with this landscape. But they relate to the farm in an extremely real way—they live off it.

September 11

I'm trying not to be so dependent on praise and appreciation. Don't really know why, perhaps because it feels
logical in terms of self-care. If you are dependent on the
judgments of others, your mood and sense of self will
be as fragile as your environment is unpredictable. But
has logic ever helped anyone? Perhaps I'm just uptight
and bad at sharing experiences and feelings with others.
A few years ago, when the flock was smaller and I was
less experienced, a crack opened in my hard exterior.
Two craftsmen, maybe electricians, were working on
something behind the barn. They had arrived early that
morning, they knew what it was they had to do. I went
down and talked to them after the children had gone to
school. Suddenly, all the sheep started bleating from the
other side of the fence, three feet away. "They recognize
you," one of the craftsmen said. "They didn't react to us
at all this morning." I felt as though I'd been seen, and
was touched.

September 12

If you don't look in on sheep regularly, they gradually become wild. They rush off and become difficult to handle. At the same time, it's relatively easy to teach them to behave themselves again.

Traditionally, I think that sheep, and other domesticated animals, were left to their own devices for much of the year. Perhaps it would be more rational to leave the flock to its own devices during the summer, meaning it would require fewer work hours . . . per pound of meat. Well, I guess that's how you calculate it.

September 13

We've bought a few more sheep for the flock. Well, I say bought; we were given them by a 4-H farm in Stockholm. Little wretches with no real future in our output, where we want a certain size and beautiful skins. But everyone's welcome. One spends her time with the young ewes and escaped today. She was on her own out on the road by the field. It's very rare that just one sheep escapes. She was stressed out and wanted to get back in again, but couldn't find a spot where she dared jump over or force her way through. We tried to corner her in the garden. She ran right past us. The second time I tricked her and she tried to jump right through me, so I managed to grab her in midair. That feeling of getting hold of a sheep that's almost completely lost its wits was something I'd forgotten. It happened a lot the first year. The flock was small, which makes the individuals edgier and less stable, and more likely to escape. I miss it a little, frankly. I carried the sheep toward the fence. It was also a long time since I'd had to lift one over the fence.

She's small, probably the smallest in the flock. These days almost all our sheep are crosses with production breeds, which makes them meatier and by this point in September, to all intents and purposes, impossible to lift over a fence. I remember an old technique. I sort of jerk the sheep away from me with her stomach over the fence so she flies right over and lands on all four legs. That way she avoids injury. Though I don't actually think sheep can injure themselves from such a low height, in some ways they're like cats physically. But it feels mean to just toss them over into the grass like a sack of potatoes. You've got to have some manners.

September 16

Still dry. The sheep have started nibbling at the tops of the nettles. That's how far it has gone. But they'll manage, they're strong.

September 25

The fence is working, no problems with the water. Salt and minerals in place. There's nothing to complain about. They walk away when I approach, but one ewe stays, lying there, as calm as an old pine. It's number 018, she's always been particularly sociable.

September 30

Times are changing on the farm. Perhaps it was unavoidable. We've started thinking of the sheep as a source of income. There are going to be even more of them, and we're going to get an accredited abattoir. We're starting to be like real farmers. You have to have an income, not be a drain on society. On the other hand, in principle you can build nuclear weapons and make porn without being a drain on society, you might even be counted as an asset in the government's math. Going around, kicking pebbles, and wondering about the meaning of everything, on the other hand, that's suspect. It's no wonder motivation's low.

October 1

These days we've rationalized the work with the sheep more and more, dividing the responsibility. I just quickly check they're alive, ideally from a distance.

There's so many other things that have to be done. Even if it was obviously annoying when they used to escape the whole time, those conflicts bound us together. The constant mucking about with the sheep gave me something to pin my existence to, something living, meaningful. Commercial meat production is meaningless. Lucrative, but meaningless.

October 18

I have to accept that the nature of our sheep management has changed. Life goes on, you have to try, feel your way forward, change. I wander around the little fold by the barn. They look at me for a few seconds before continuing to graze. Even some of the older ewes, who've seen me here almost every day of their lives, seem to wonder for a moment if I'm a predator or some other danger. At the beginning of my time with the sheep there was a lot of this—standing and watching and thinking. Now it's more like a job. It doesn't seem possible to stop that process. I don't know what it is, but that simple way of being a shepherd and experiencing the sheep's way of life sort of lacks force. It's like the lamb that can't get food from the ewe, it fades away slowly. At the same time, the actual relationship to the sheep and their unassuming existence is still there. The fence, the grass, the bleating, the rumination. Commercial meat production might take my time and my work, but it won't take my thoughts.

October 19

The guy herding the sheep is having problems with 018. She's attacking the dogs. He wants to cull her; we can't have these genes being passed down if we want a functioning flock. She comes over to me in the field. "I think we can hold them off," I whisper.